D1413516

WATER

GOES ROUND

THE WATER CYCLE

BY
ROBIN KOONTZ

ILLUSTRATED BY
CHRIS DAVIDSON

Consultant:
Mark Green, PhD
Assistant Professor of Hydrology
Plymouth State University
Plymouth, New Hampshire

CAPSTONE PRESS
a capstone imprint

First Graphics are published by Capstone Press,
1710 Roe Crest Drive, North Mankato, Minnesota 56003.
www.capstonepub.com

Books published by Capstone Press are manufactured with paper
containing at least 10 percent post-consumer waste.

Library of Congress Cataloging-in-Publication Data
Koontz, Robin Michal.
  Water goes round : the water cycle / by Robin Koontz ;
illustrated by Chris Davidson.
    p. cm.—(First graphics. Nature cycles)
  Includes bibliographical references and index.
  Summary: "In graphic novel format, text and illustrations describe the key stages
of the water cycle"—Provided by publisher.
  ISBN 978-1-4296-5364-0 (library binding)
  ISBN 978-1-4296-6231-4 (paperback)
  1. Hydrologic cycle—Juvenile literature. 2. Hydrologic cycle—Comic books, strips,
etc.—Juvenile literature. I. Davidson, Chris, 1974– ill. II. Title. III. Series.

  GB848.K66 2011
  551.48—dc22   2010030093

Editor: *Christopher L. Harbo*
Designer: *Lori Bye*
Art Director: *Nathan Gassman*
Production Specialist: *Eric Manske*

Printed in the United States of America in North Mankato, Minnesota.
032012   006648R

Table of Contents

Water, Water Everywhere

Water covers most of the planet.

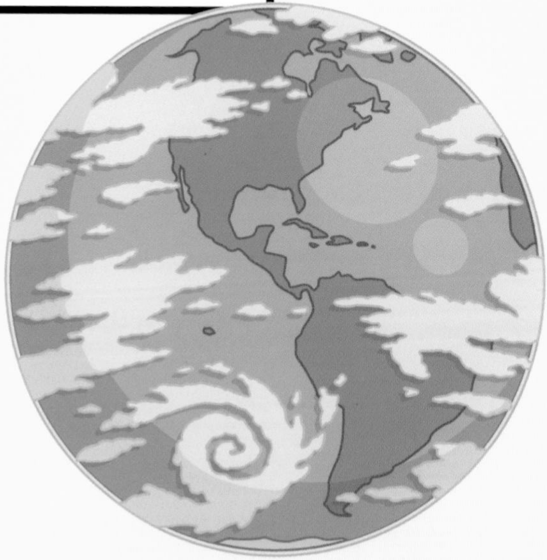

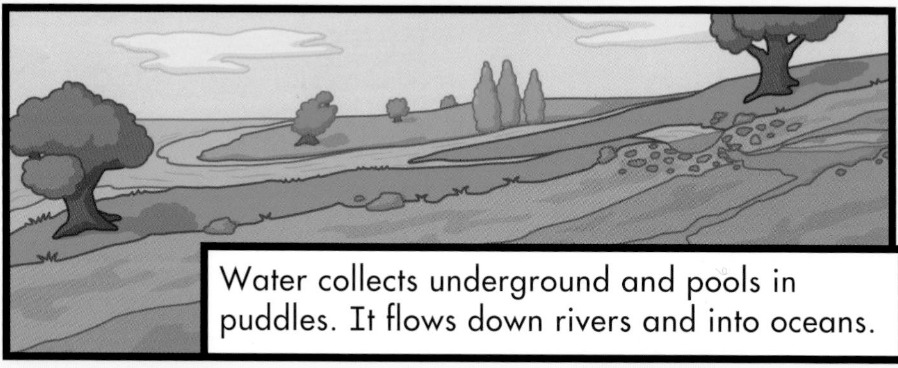

Water collects underground and pools in puddles. It flows down rivers and into oceans.

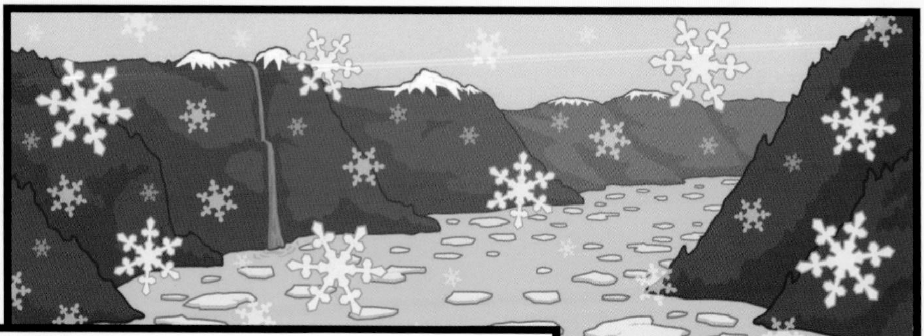

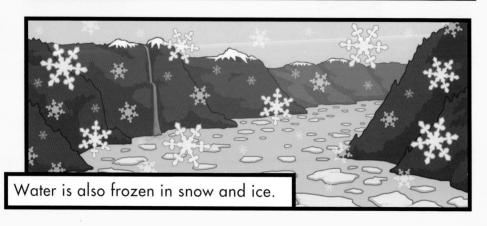

Water is also frozen in snow and ice.

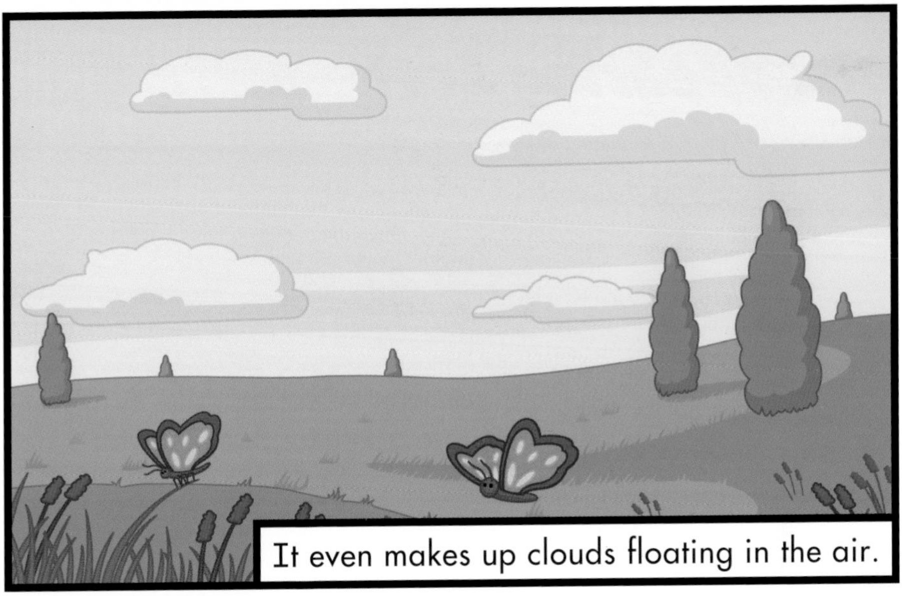
It even makes up clouds floating in the air.

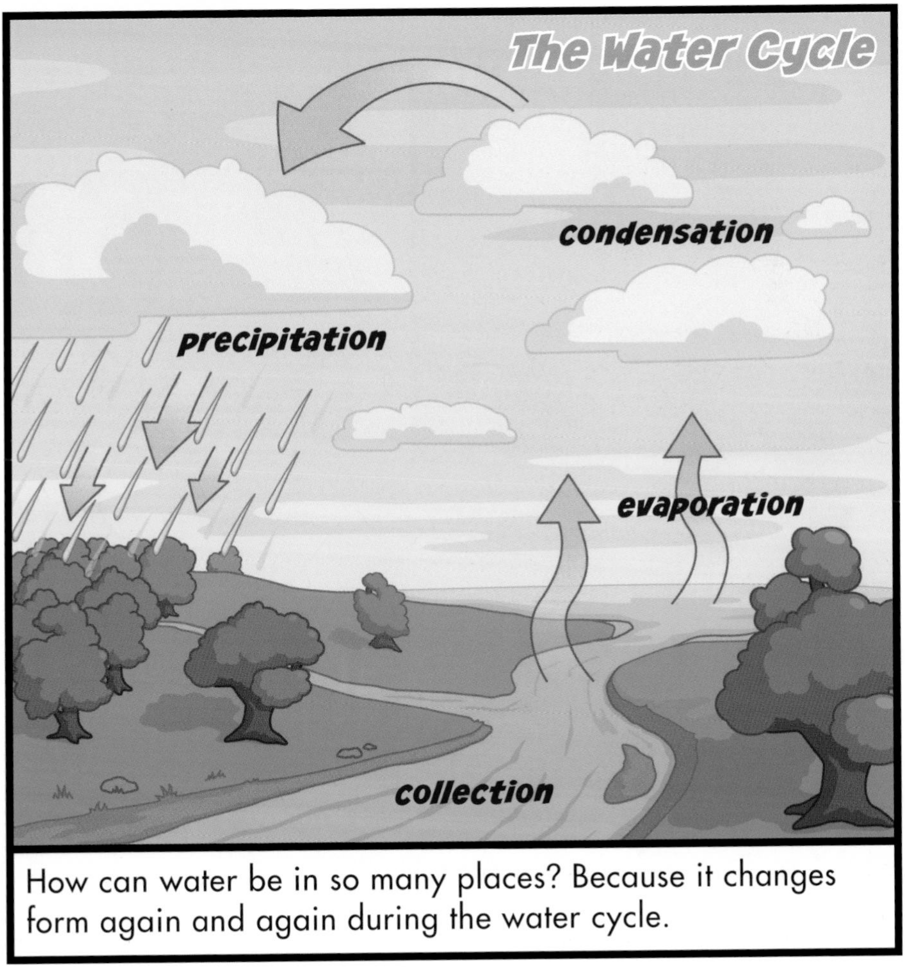
The Water Cycle
condensation
precipitation
evaporation
collection
How can water be in so many places? Because it changes form again and again during the water cycle.

Disappearing Act!

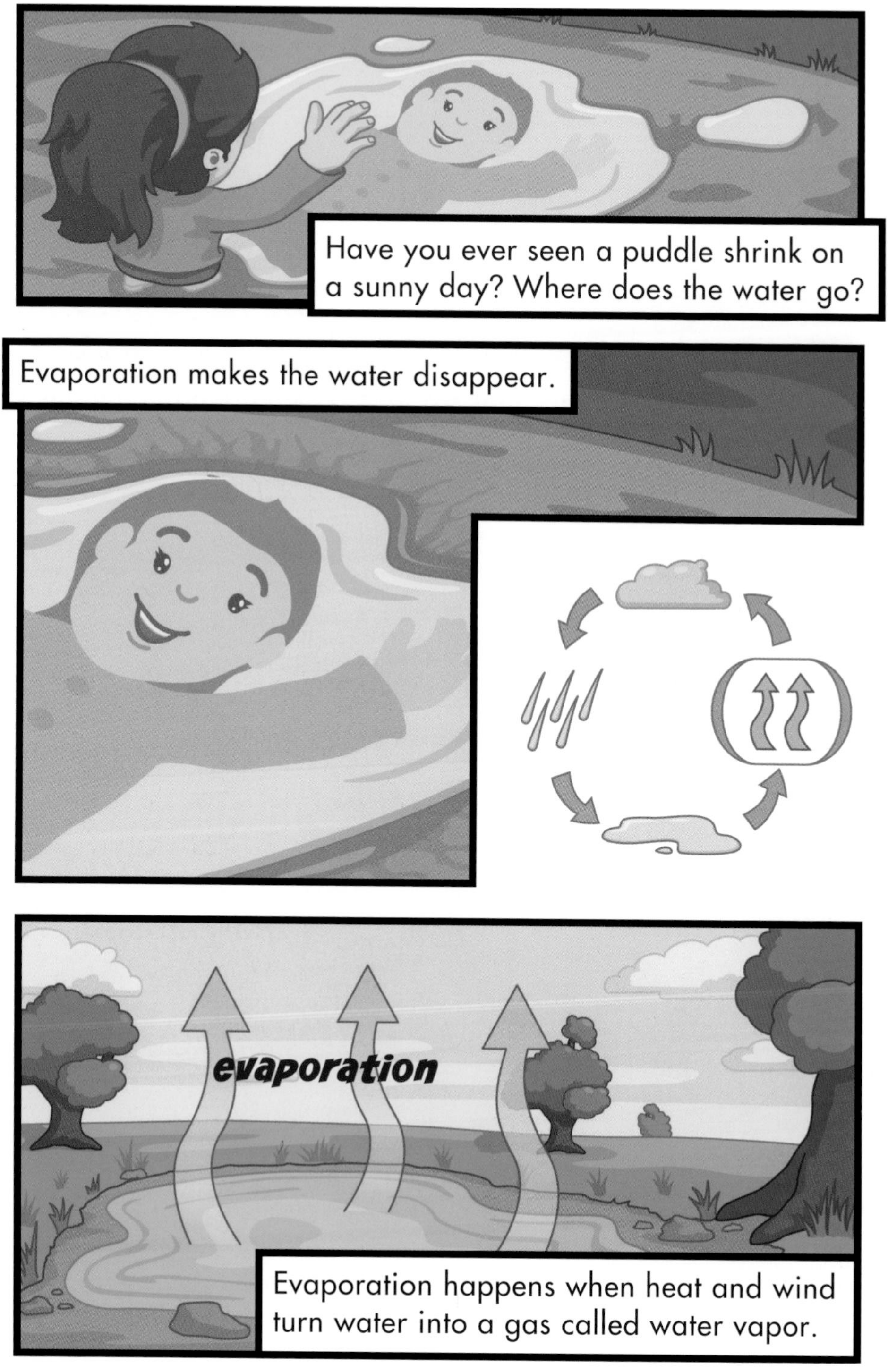
Have you ever seen a puddle shrink on a sunny day? Where does the water go?
Evaporation makes the water disappear.
evaporation
Evaporation happens when heat and wind turn water into a gas called water vapor.

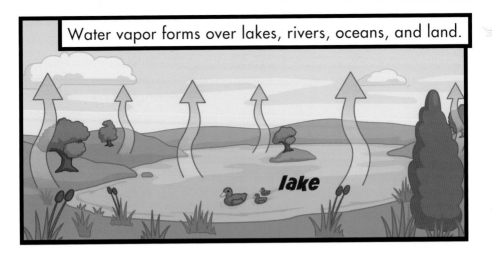
Water vapor forms over lakes, rivers, oceans, and land.

Wind carries water vapor into the air. The water vapor cools as it rises.

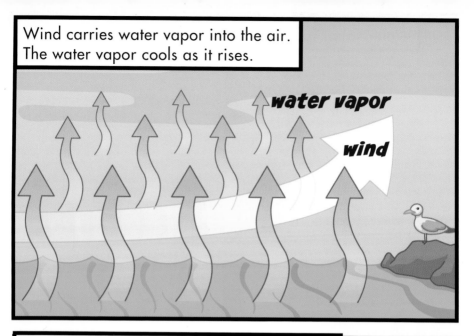

This cooling causes condensation. Condensation changes water vapor back to a liquid. Tiny water droplets form in the air.

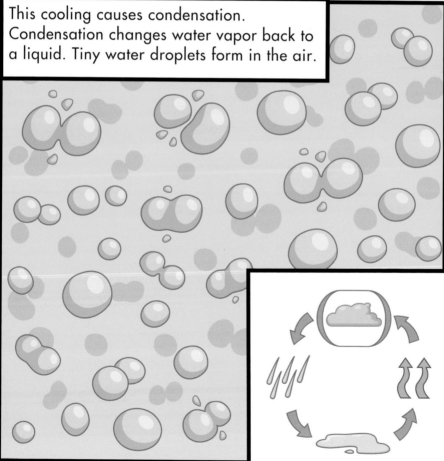

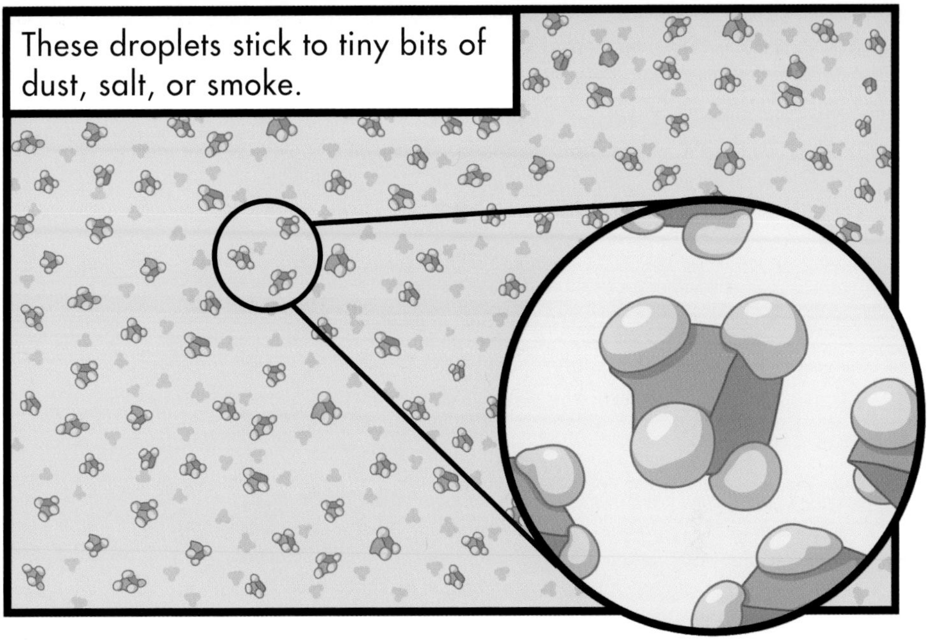
These droplets stick to tiny bits of dust, salt, or smoke.

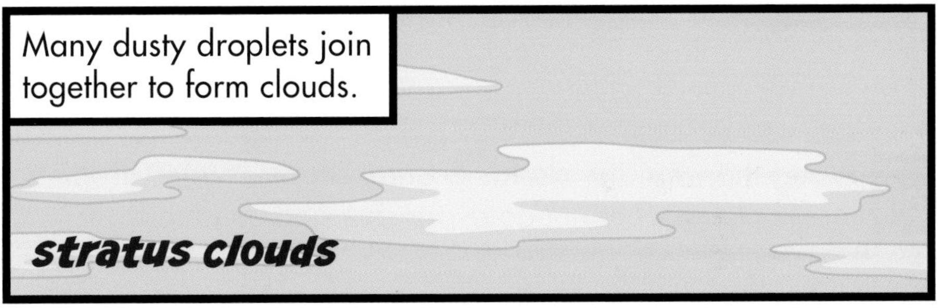
Many dusty droplets join together to form clouds.
stratus clouds

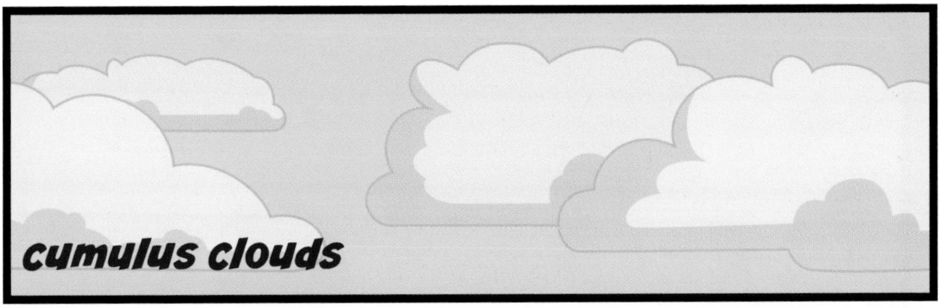
cumulus clouds

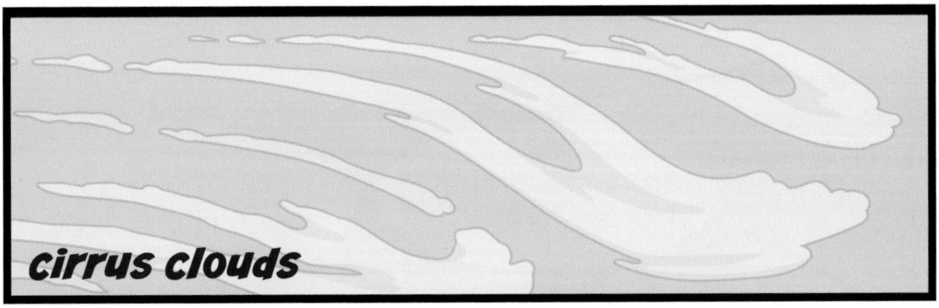
cirrus clouds

Clouds carry water around the globe.

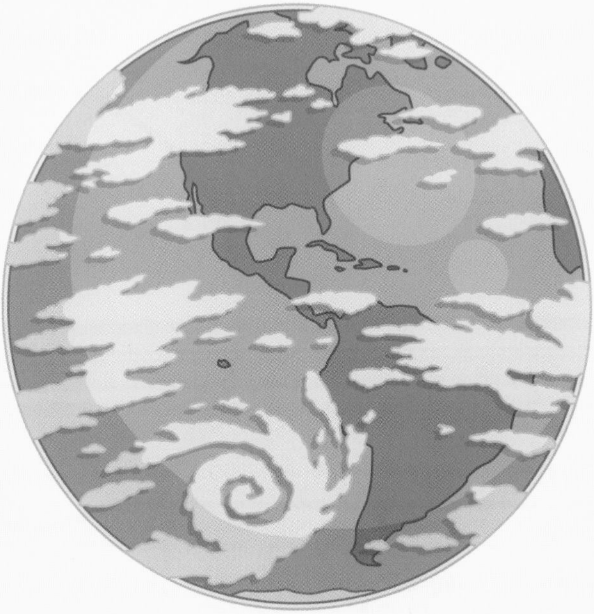

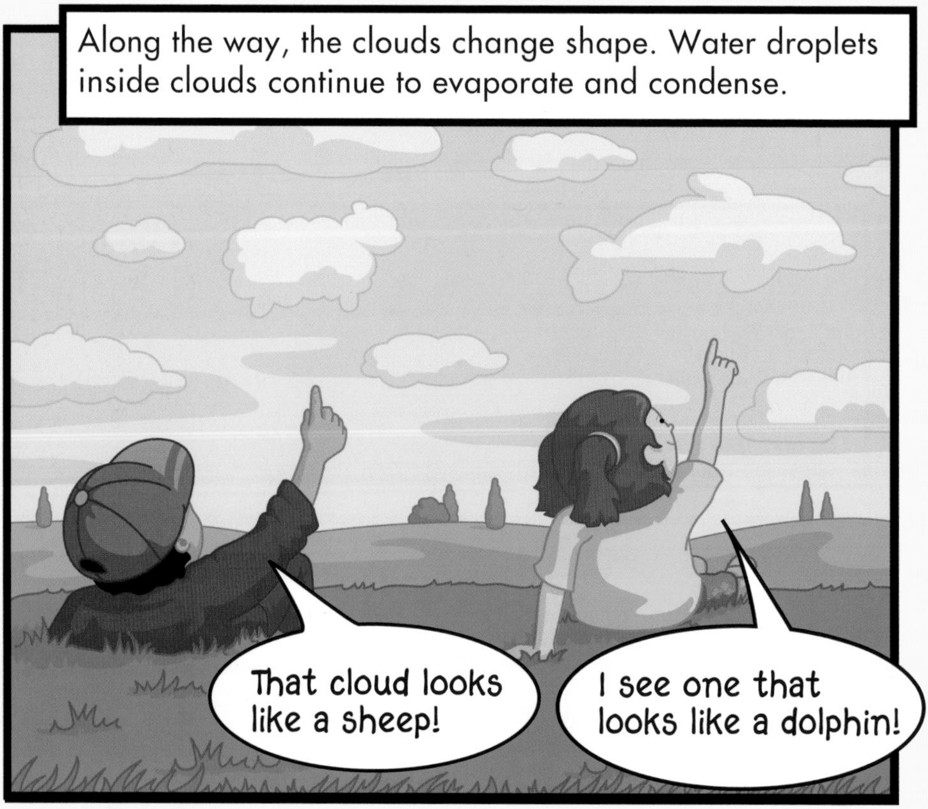
Along the way, the clouds change shape. Water droplets inside clouds continue to evaporate and condense.
That cloud looks like a sheep!
I see one that looks like a dolphin!

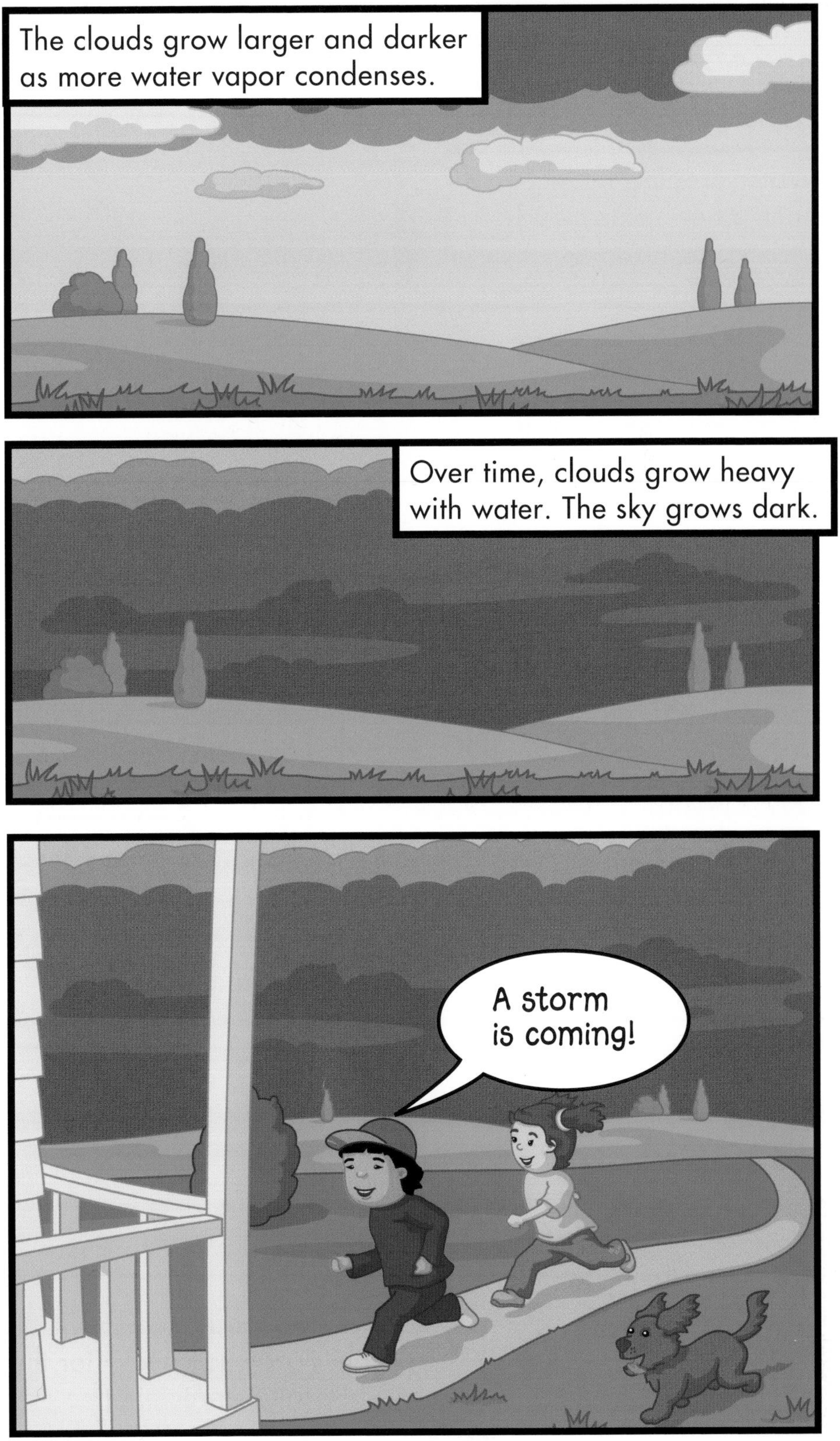
The clouds grow larger and darker as more water vapor condenses.
Over time, clouds grow heavy with water. The sky grows dark.
A storm is coming!

What Goes Up Must Come Down

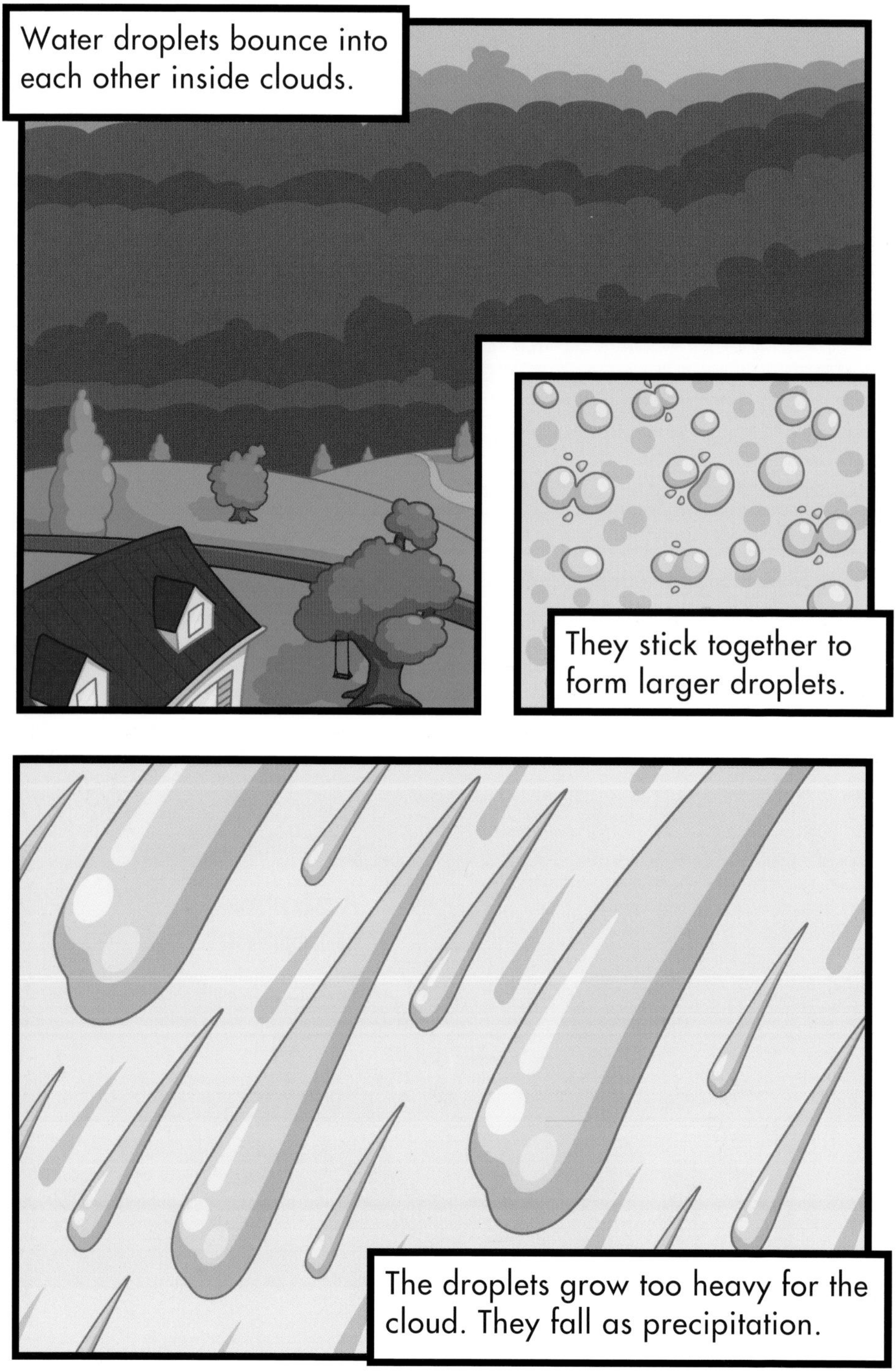
Water droplets bounce into each other inside clouds.
They stick together to form larger droplets.
The droplets grow too heavy for the cloud. They fall as precipitation.

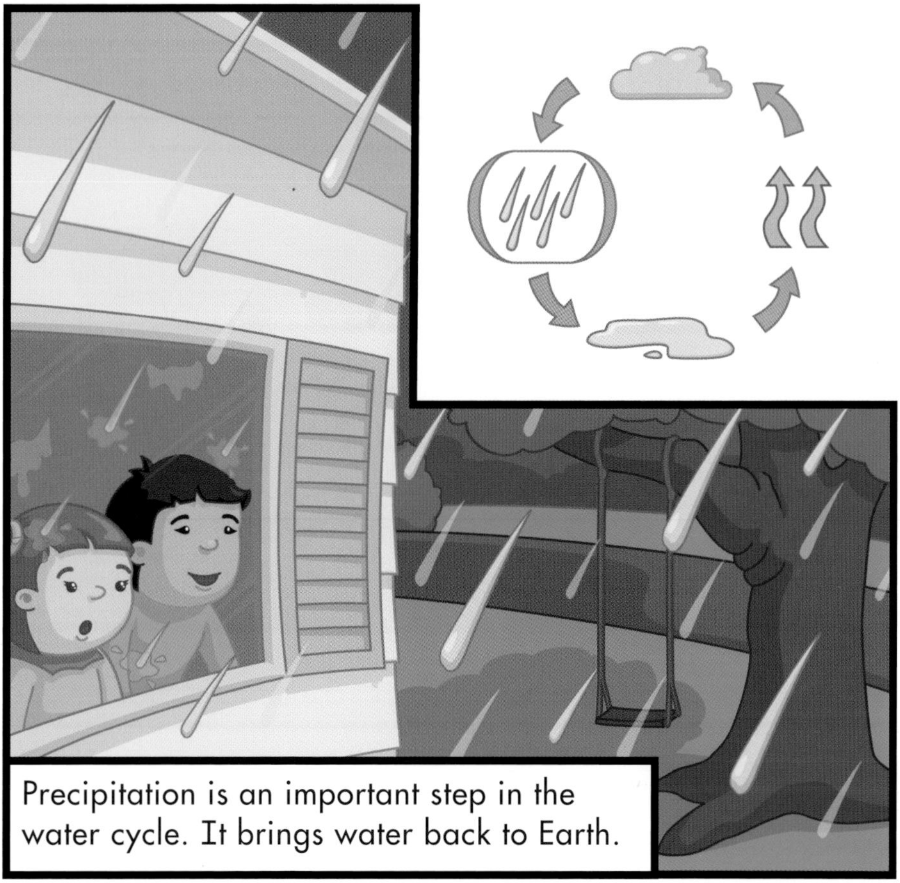
Precipitation is an important step in the water cycle. It brings water back to Earth.

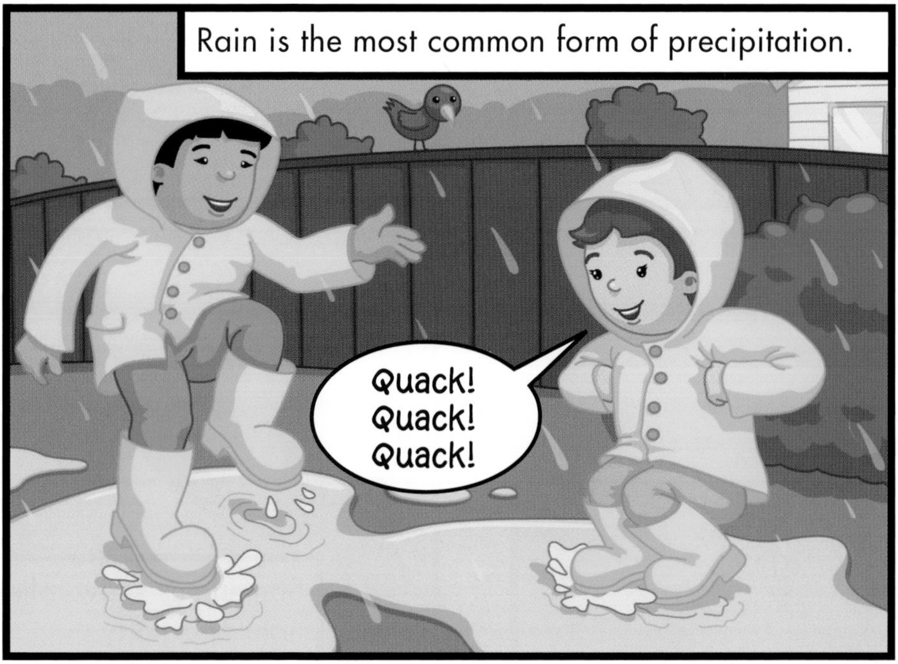
Rain is the most common form of precipitation.
Quack! Quack! Quack!

Rain is only one form of precipitation. Water droplets freeze at 32 degrees Fahrenheit (0 degrees Celsius). They fall as snow, sleet, or hail.

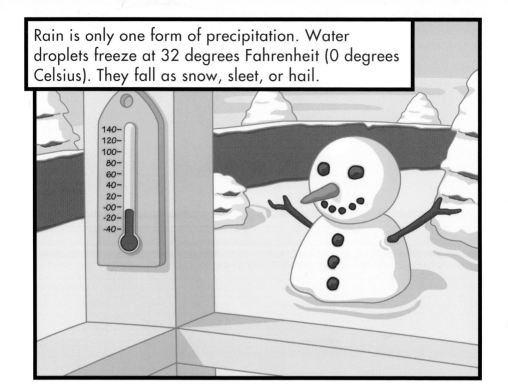

Snowflakes form when water droplets freeze and stick together in the clouds.

Sometimes snow falls light and fluffy.

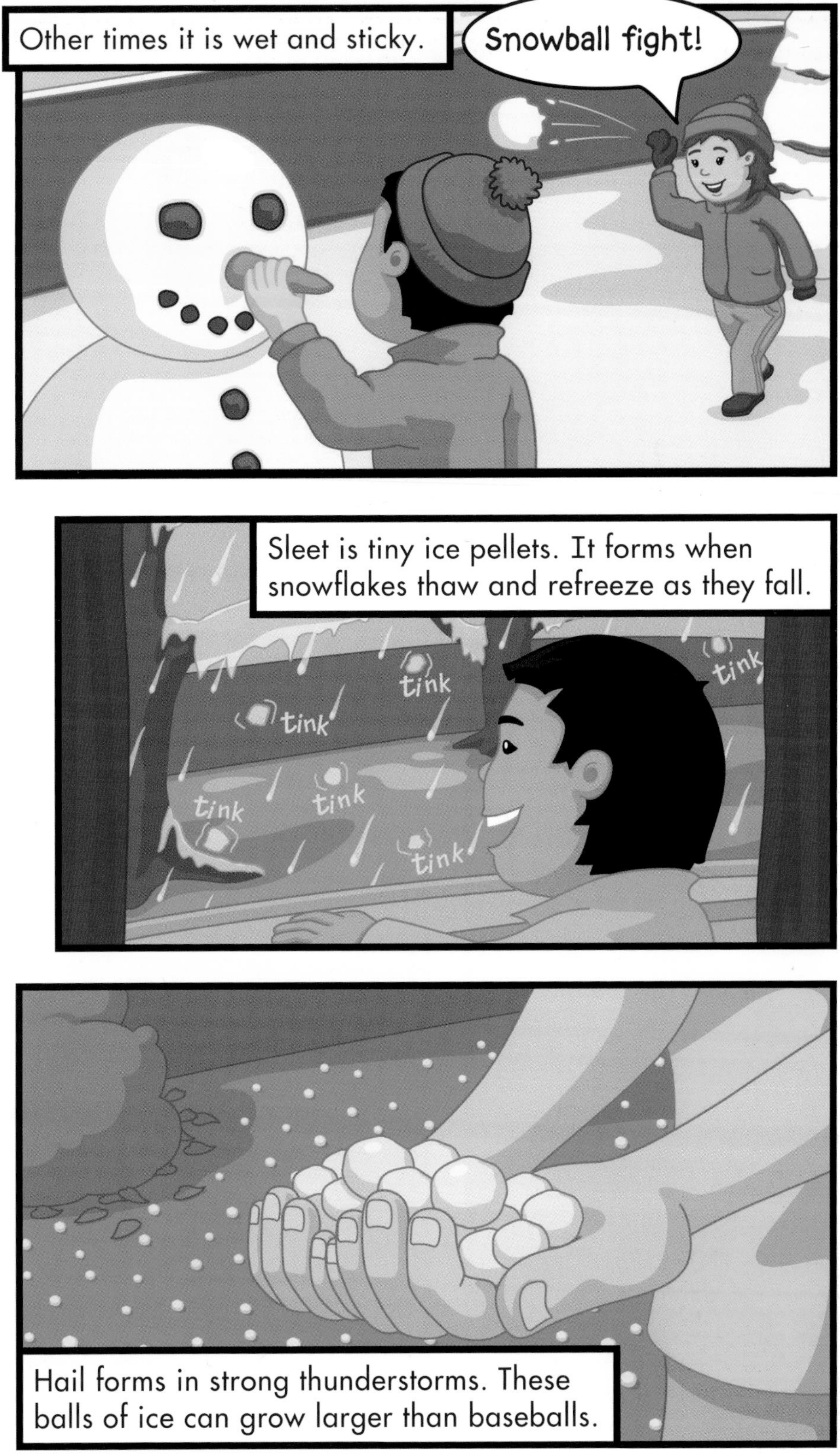
Other times it is wet and sticky.
Snowball fight!
Sleet is tiny ice pellets. It forms when snowflakes thaw and refreeze as they fall.
tink
tink
tink
tink
tink
tink
Hail forms in strong thunderstorms. These balls of ice can grow larger than baseballs.

A Gathering of Drops

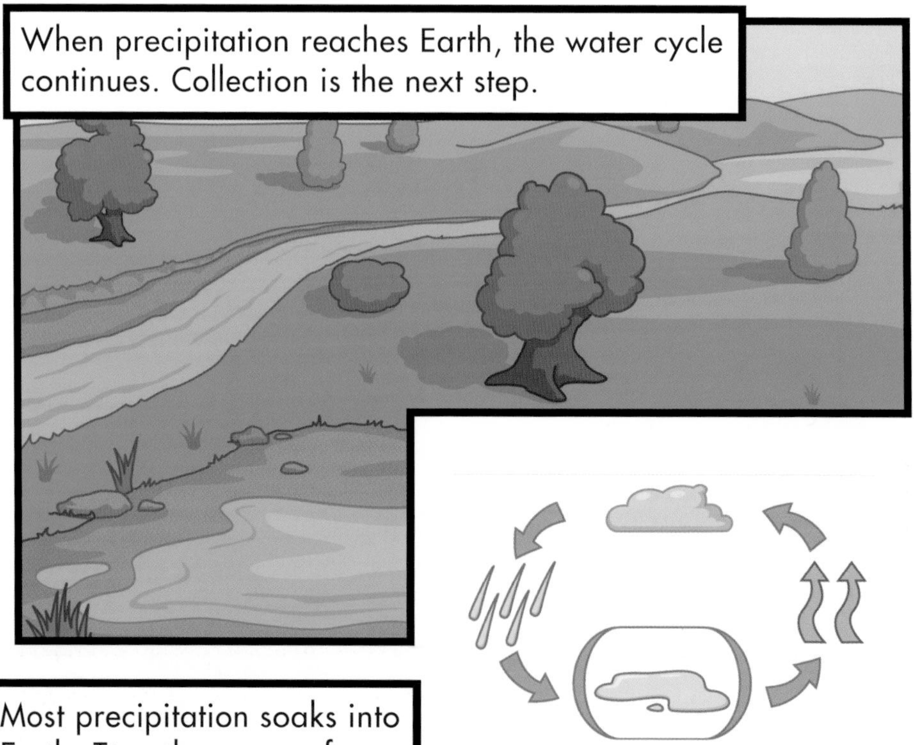
When precipitation reaches Earth, the water cycle continues. Collection is the next step.

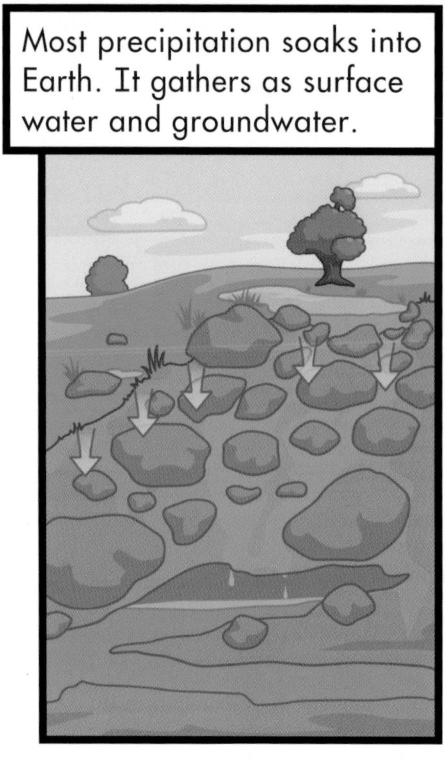
Most precipitation soaks into Earth. It gathers as surface water and groundwater.

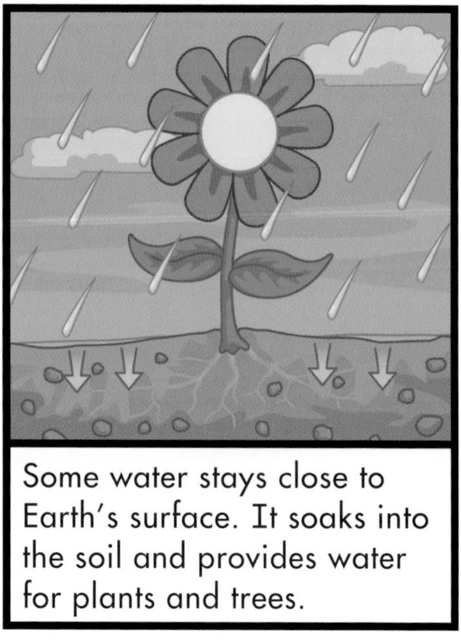
Some water stays close to Earth's surface. It soaks into the soil and provides water for plants and trees.

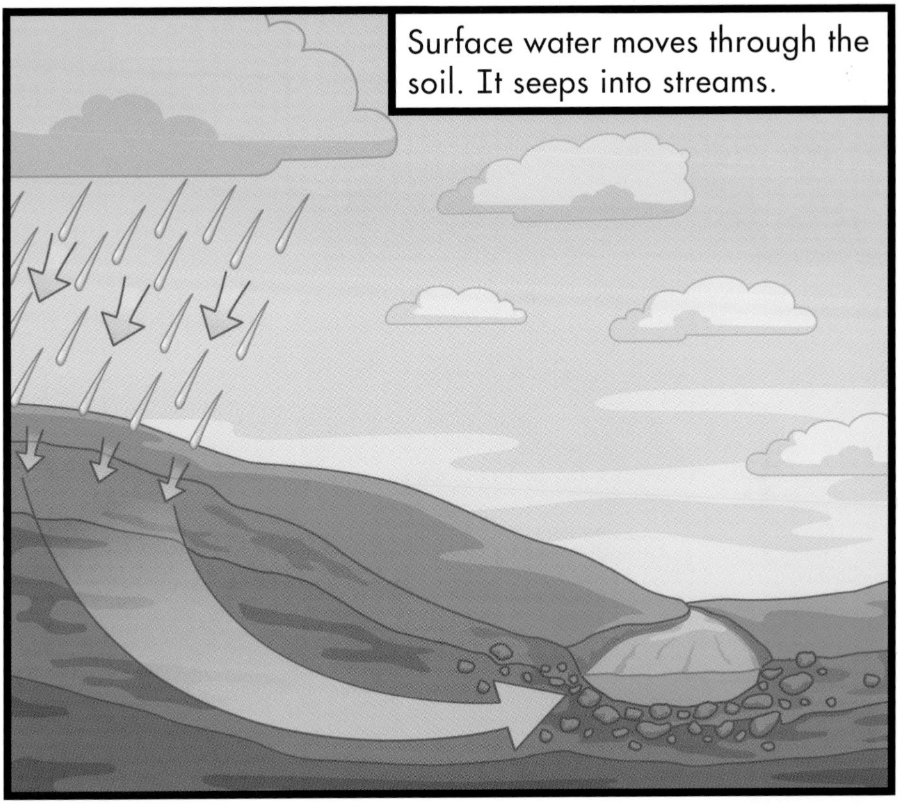
Surface water moves through the soil. It seeps into streams.

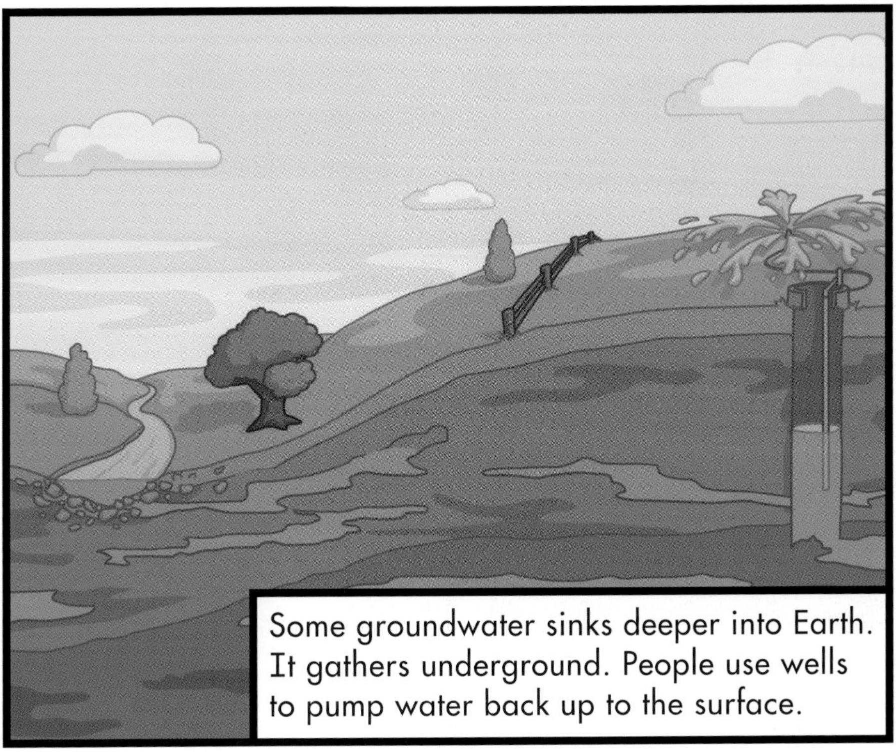
Some groundwater sinks deeper into Earth. It gathers underground. People use wells to pump water back up to the surface.

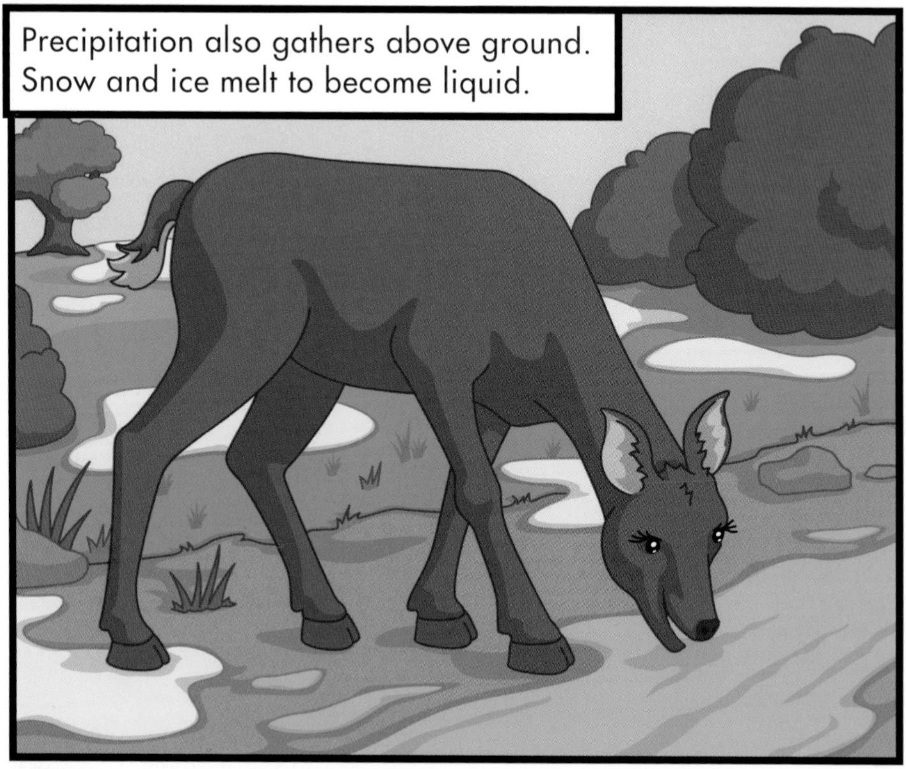
Precipitation also gathers above ground. Snow and ice melt to become liquid.

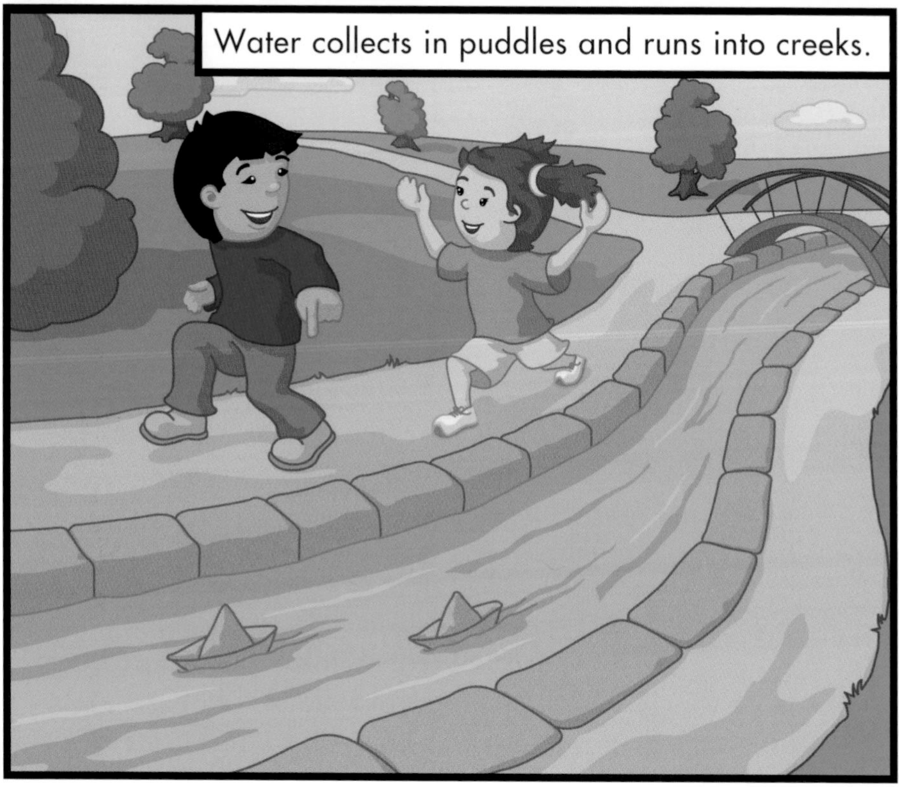
Water collects in puddles and runs into creeks.

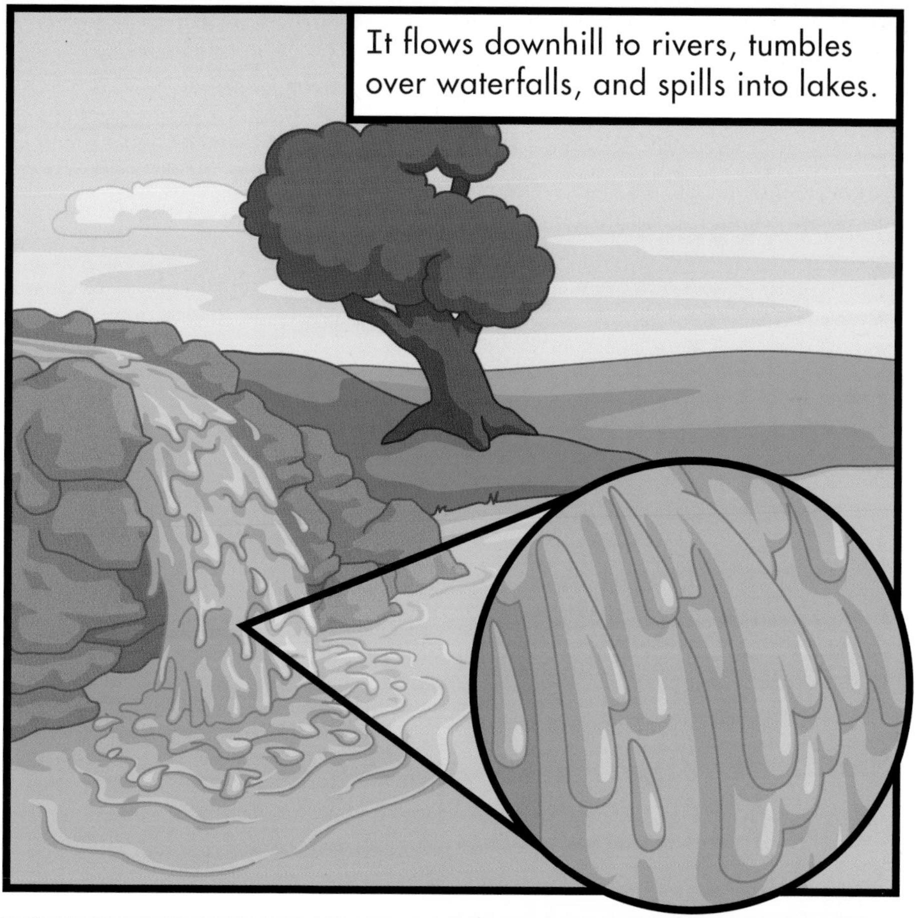
It flows downhill to rivers, tumbles over waterfalls, and spills into lakes.

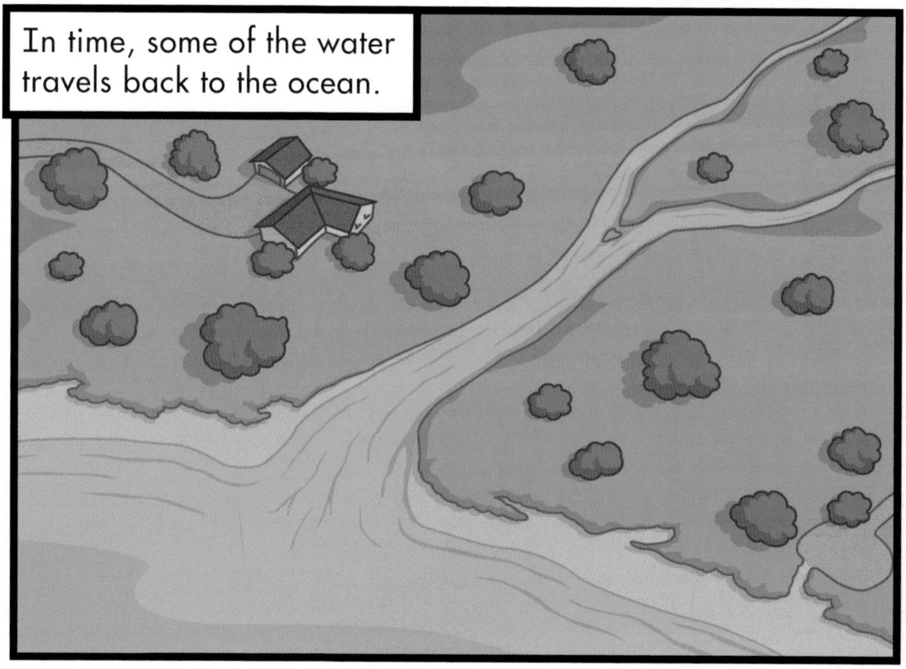
In time, some of the water travels back to the ocean.

An Endless Water Cycle

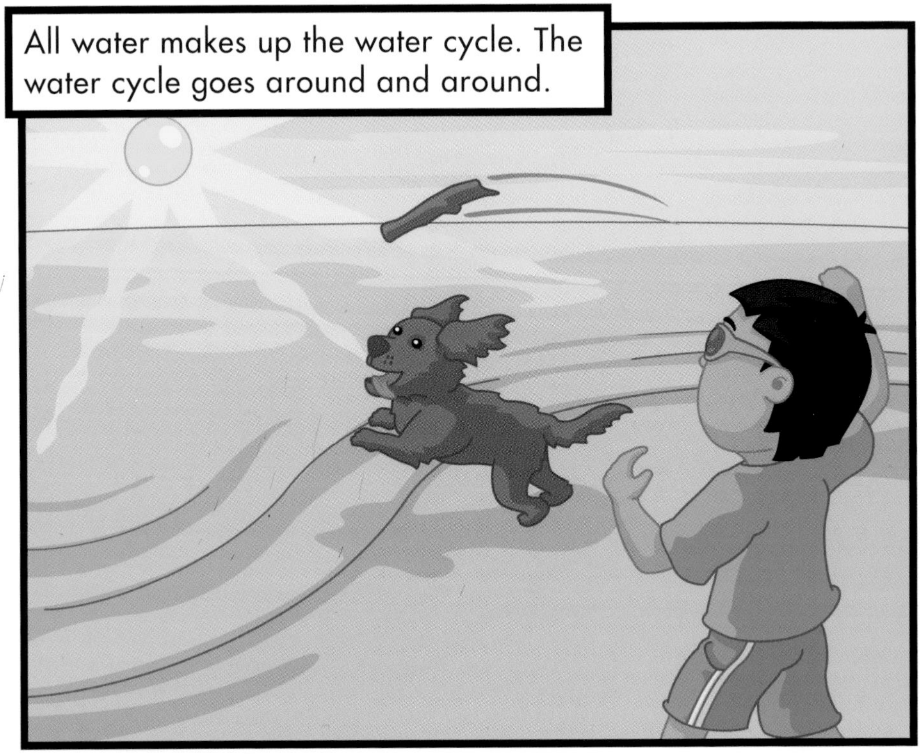
All water makes up the water cycle. The water cycle goes around and around.

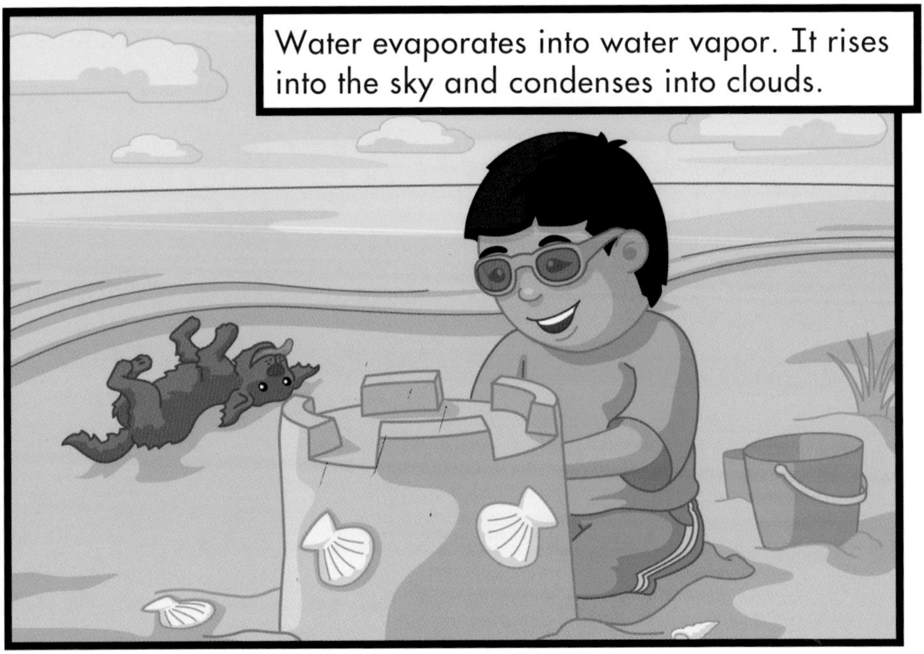
Water evaporates into water vapor. It rises into the sky and condenses into clouds.

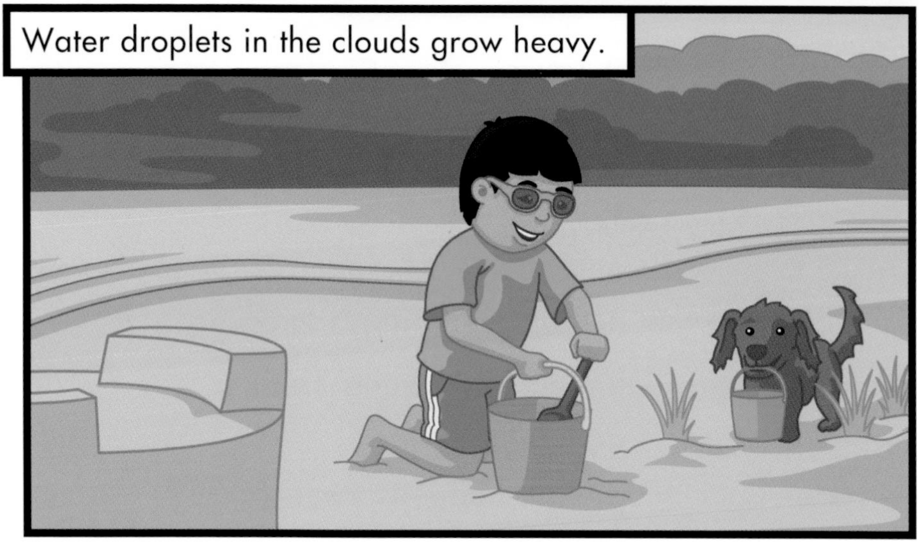
Water droplets in the clouds grow heavy.

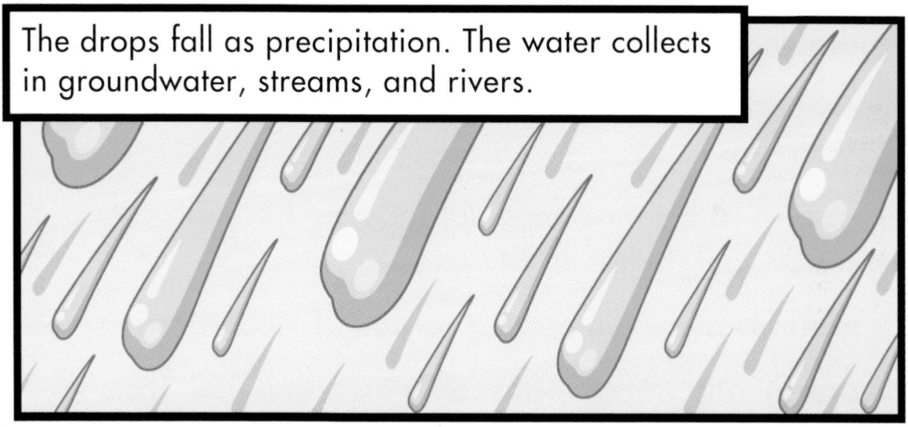
The drops fall as precipitation. The water collects in groundwater, streams, and rivers.

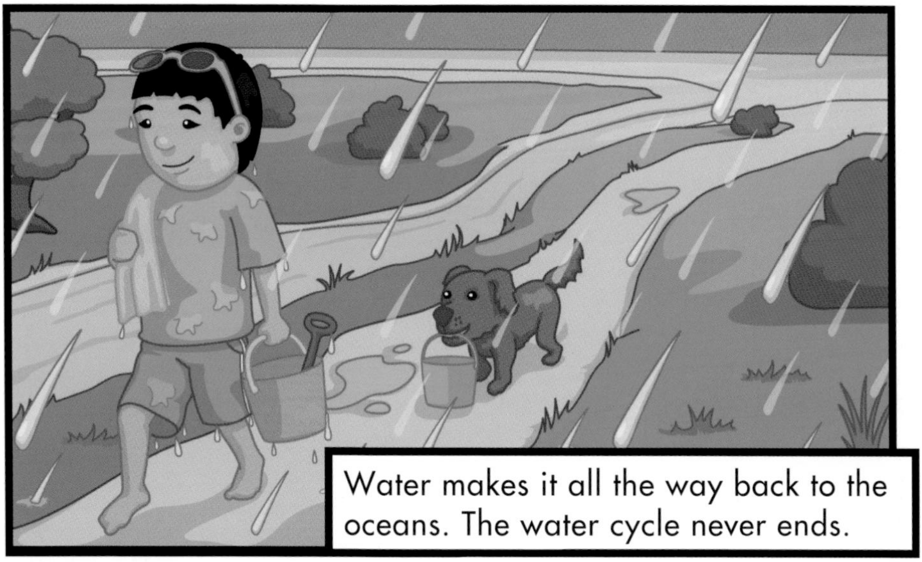
Water makes it all the way back to the oceans. The water cycle never ends.

Glossary

collection—the act of gathering something

condensation—the act of turning from a gas into a liquid

cycle—something that happens over and over again

droplet—a very small drop of liquid

evaporation—the act of turning from a liquid to a gas

gas—a substance that spreads to fill any space that holds it

groundwater—water that is found underground

precipitation—all forms of water that fall from clouds; forms of precipitation include rain, snow, and hail

vapor—a gas made from a liquid

Read More

Bauman, Amy. *Earth's Water Cycle*. Planet Earth. Pleasantville, N.Y.: Gareth Stevens Pub., 2008.

Flynn, Claire E. *Water World: Earth's Water Cycle*. New York: PowerKids Press, 2009.

Green, Jen. *How the Water Cycle Works*. Our Earth. New York: PowerKids Press, 2008.

Rau, Dana Meachen. *Water*. Nature's Cycles. New York: Marshall Cavendish Benchmark, 2009.

Internet Sites

FactHound offers a safe, fun way to find Internet sites related to this book. All of the sites on FactHound have been researched by our staff.

Here's all you do:

Visit *www.facthound.com*

Type in this code: 9781429653640

Check out projects, games and lots more at
www.capstonekids.com

23

Index

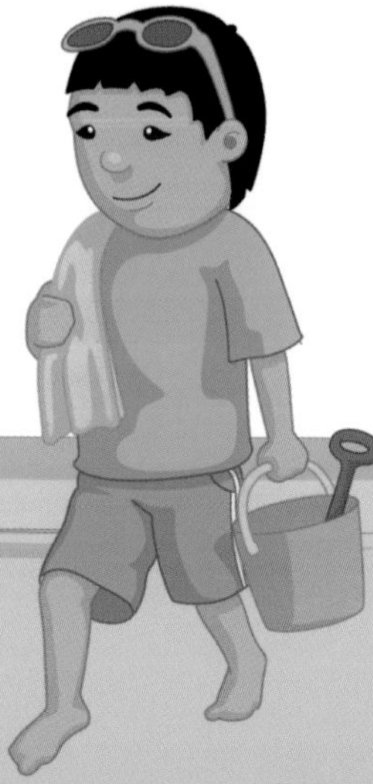

TITLES IN THIS SET:

EGGS, LEGS, WINGS
A Butterfly Life Cycle

HIDE and SEEK MOON
The Moon Phases

SEED, SPROUT, FRUIT
An Apple Tree Life Cycle

WATER GOES ROUND
The Water Cycle